True Tales o

Daring Pony Express Riders

Jeff Savage

Enslow Publishers, Inc.
40 Industrial Road
Box 398
Berkeley Heights, NJ 07922
USA

http://www.enslow.com

Copyright © 2012 by Jeff Savage

All rights reserved.

No part of this book may be reproduced by any means
without the written permission of the Publisher.

Original edition published as *Pony Express Riders of the Wild West* in 1995.

Library of Congress Cataloging-in-Publication Data

Savage, Jeff, 1961–
    Daring Pony Express riders : true tales of the Wild West / Jeff Savage.
      p. cm. — (True tales of the Wild West)
    "Original edition published as Pony Express Riders of the Wild West in 1995."
    Includes bibliographical references and index.
    Summary: "Examines the Pony Express, including the origins of the mail carrier
  service, the trails and stations, the Pony Express riders, amazing stories from the
  riders, and the legacy of the Pony Express"—Provided by publisher.
    ISBN 978-0-7660-4023-6
    1. Pony express—History—Juvenile literature. 2. Postal service—United
States—History—19th century—Juvenile literature. 3. West (U.S.)—History—
Juvenile literature. I. Savage, Jeff, 1961– Pony express riders of the Wild West.
II. Title.
    HE6375.P65S28 2012
    383'.143092273—dc23   2011028124

Paperback ISBN 978-1-4644-0031-5
ePUB ISBN 978-1-4645-0476-1
PDF ISBN 978-1-4646-0476-8

Printed in the United States of America

092011 Lake Book Manufacturing, Inc., Melrose Park, IL

10 9 8 7 6 5 4 3 2 1

To Our Readers: We have done our best to make sure all Internet addresses in this book
were active and appropriate when we went to press. However, the author and the
Publisher have no control over, and assume no liability for, the material available on
those Internet sites or on other Web sites they may link to. Any comments or suggestions
can be sent by e-mail to comments@enslow.com or to the address on the back cover.

Enslow Publishers, Inc., is committed to printing our books on recycled paper. The
paper in every book contains 10% to 30% post-consumer waste (PCW). The cover
board on the outside of each book contains 100% PCW. Our goal is to do our part to
help young people and the environment too!

Illustration Credits: Bettmann/Getty Images, p. 17; Buffalo Bill Historical Center,
Cody, Wyoming, U.S.A., Garlow Collection, P.69.2078, p. 28; © Corel Corporation, p.
30; Enslow Publishers, Inc., p. 15; © Enslow Publishers, Inc. / Paul Daly, p. 1;
Keystone/Hulton Archive/Getty Images, p. 20; Library of Congress Prints and
Photographs Division, p. 35, 41; National Archives, pp. 6, 42; © North Wind Picture
Archives, p. 33; Wells Fargo Bank, N.A., pp. 10, 23.

Cover Illustration: © Enslow Publishers, Inc. / Paul Daly.

Contents

Chapter 1
The Mail Must and Will Go Through 5

Chapter 2
A Great Express Adventure 12

Chapter 3
The Adventure Begins 18

Chapter 4
"Young Skinny Wiry Fellows" 25

Chapter 5
Overcoming the Wilderness 32

Chapter 6
Farewell and Forever 39

Chapter Notes 43

Glossary 45

Further Reading
(Books and Internet Addresses) 47

Index 48

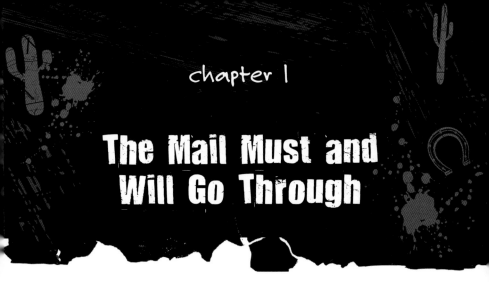

chapter 1

The Mail Must and Will Go Through

Bob Haslam gazed across the horizon as thin columns of smoke rose from the east. The Paiute were at war—attacking the settlers who were invading their land. They were setting fire to homes, stealing horses, and killing when they could.

Bob stood outside Friday's Station, a log building at the southern tip of Lake Tahoe. To the west was California, where a nearby relay station had been raided the day before. To the east lay Nevada, where the Paiute were out in full force.

Bob waited nervously at the station for the rider to arrive with the mochila, the Pony Express mailbag. His horse stood nearby, freshly watered and ready to go. It was one of the fastest horses in the region. The Pony Express used only the best. Bob was so famous for being a courageous rider that he was known simply

This photo of a Pony Express rider was taken in 1861. Pony Bob Haslam was one of many young riders who faced danger every day carrying mail for the Pony Express.

as Pony Bob. With the Paiute on the attack, he would need every ounce of his courage to make it through this trip.

The rider was late with the mochila. Pony Bob began to worry. The station keeper suggested that maybe the rider had been killed by Paiute warriors. Pony Bob refused to believe it.

Eventually, Bob saw what he had hoped for: a cloud of dust in the distance, coming his way. It had to be Tom King! Within moments, Tom was spurring his horse into the station.

Pony Bob grabbed the mochila from Tom and threw it over his own horse's saddle. "Maybe you'd better stick around, Bob," the station keeper said. "I'd say you got no more chance of reaching Bucklands than reaching the moon." Not a chance, Bob thought. The mail had to get through. "So long," he shouted as he mounted his pony and dashed off.[1]

Pony Bob changed horses twice along the way, reaching Reed's Station in good time. Now his journey to Bucklands was almost complete. To his dismay, there was no fresh horse waiting for him at Reed's Station. All the animals were being used in the battle with the Paiute. Bob had no choice but to feed his weary horse and then go. He galloped along the Carson River as fast as his tired horse could take him, until he reached Bucklands.

Pony Bob was exhausted when he arrived at the station. He had traveled nearly eighty miles. To his surprise, there was no rider outside waiting for him. Bob jumped off his horse and ran into the station. Inside he found W. C. Marley, the station keeper, and the next rider, Johnny Richardson, sitting at a table playing cards.

"Say, aren't you riding?" Pony Bob asked.

"No, I'm sick," Johnny answered.

"He's yellow, scared of Injuns," said the station keeper.[2]

Pony Bob and Marley did their best to persuade Johnny to ride. It was no use.

Marley knew that the mail had to get through to Smith's Creek. He turned to Pony Bob and said, "Bob, I will give you fifty dollars if you make this ride." Bob stood up straight. "I will go at once," he replied.[3]

Armed with a Colt revolver and Spencer rifle, Pony Bob grabbed the mochila, mounted a fresh horse, and sped off. He was weary, his bones ached, and it was getting dark. Smith's Creek was more than 130 miles away. How would he ever make it?

Sink of the Carson was his first stop. He changed to a fresh horse and went on. He had ninety miles to go. Bob wasn't just concerned about Paiute anymore; he was trying to hang onto his horse. He pushed on over alkali wastes and through the sand, going thirty miles without a drop of water, until he reached Sand Springs, his second relay station. Here again he changed horses and dashed on once more.

Bob was so fatigued at this point that he didn't notice his horse perk up its ears in alarm. Yells rang out; the Paiute were attacking! Pony Bob crouched down in the saddle and spurred his horse on. Arrows flew through the air, and guns roared. Bob hung tight to his horse, and in seconds he made it past the Paiute warriors. Shots rang out. Bob looked behind him and saw several Paiute on horses chasing him. He ducked down and drove his horse faster.

Pony Bob's horse was as quick as lightning, but the Paiute kept up. Bob looked back and saw them right on his tail. He couldn't understand it. How could those horses keep up with his carefully selected Pony Express steed? Then he remembered. Relay stations across the line had been raided in recent weeks. These were stolen Pony Express horses!

The Paiute drew closer. Pony Bob grabbed his pistol, spun around, and fired at them. One man went down. The others closed in. They returned fire. The courageous rider felt a sharp pain surge through his shoulder. He had been hit! Bob's arm dropped to his side. Another bullet grazed his cheek.

Pony Bob maintained his furious pace, and soon the shooting stopped. He looked back; the Paiute were gone. He trotted into Cold Springs a bloodied figure. The station keeper took one look at him and said, "You're in no shape to ride. Bill or me will take the

In this illustration, Pony Bob races away from American Indian attackers during a journey from Smith's Creek to Fort Churchill, Nevada, while carrying the presidential election returns of 1860. Abraham Lincoln was elected president that year.

mochila on."[4] Pony Bob would not be denied. "Get me a horse," he demanded. "I'm going through."[5]

Bob wrapped a towel around his arm and rode to Smith's Creek, where relief rider J. G. Kelley was waiting. Bob handed the mailbag over, and Kelley was off in a flash. Pony Bob collapsed, exhausted, in the station house.

The adventure didn't end there. It seemed that he had hardly slept when the station keeper awakened him. The rider heading back to the west had come in, and was unable to continue. He had broken his leg when he was thrown from his horse.

"He stays, but not the mochila," Pony Bob said as he rose from his bed. "That mail's got to go through. I'm riding!"[6]

Bob staggered outside to a fresh horse, climbed aboard with one arm dangling uselessly at his side, and rode off. Through the darkness he galloped, retracing the route he had just covered. Wolves howled around him.

Bob arrived at Cold Springs to find that the station had just been burned to the ground. The station keeper and the replacement horse lay on the ground, killed by arrows. Frightened, Bob urged his horse on. The wolves kept howling. Bob knew the Paiute could attack him at any moment.

Somehow, he made it back to Sink of the Carson, to Bucklands, and on to Friday's—his home station. Tom King took the mail from there and headed west with it to Sacramento. Pony Bob was so drained that he had to be helped off his horse and carried inside. He had traveled some 380 miles with little rest. He was such a hero that the Pony Express Company gave him another fifty-dollar bonus. Pony Bob accepted the reward money, but not the praise. After all, *the mail must and will go through.*

chapter 2

A Great Express Adventure

The discovery of gold in 1848 brought thousands of people to California. Once in the Golden State, these newly arrived immigrants sent word to their families back east describing the beauty of the land. More and more people came. Getting word back to the Easterners was hard, and people in the West needed a way to get news from back home.

The only reliable coast-to-coast connection was the steamship. Letters were transported from the East by boat down the Atlantic coast, around the tip of South America, and up the Pacific coast to California and Oregon. The trip was halved when a fifty-mile railroad track was laid across the Isthmus of Panama. Still, it took about one month for a letter to make its way from coast to coast—much too slow for people in the West. Many of them had traveled from the East in wagons. Why couldn't the mail come overland as they did?

Sure enough, by 1851, the mail was being transported in stagecoaches. The Butterfield Overland Mail Company, named after its founder, John Butterfield, took mail across the southern states, from St. Louis to San Diego. A central route came later, followed by a northern route. Meanwhile, people continued to pour into the West. By 1860, California's population was 380,000. Overland mail routes were refined. More stations were established. Still, the mail was slow.

An Idea Is Born

It was around this time, in early 1860, that a businessman named William H. Russell had an idea. Russell would compete with the Overland Mail Company by creating a network of pony riders that could carry the mail faster. In a letter to a business partner, William B. Waddell, Russell wrote that he wanted "to build a world-wide reputation, even at considerable expense and also to incur large expenses in many ways, the details of which I cannot commit to paper."[1] Together with a third partner, Alexander Majors, Waddell and Russell spent a total of $100,000 to create the Pony Express. Another $600,000 would be spent to maintain it.

The trio of Russell, Majors, and Waddell chose to use a route from St. Joseph, Missouri, to Sacramento, California. The telegraph was in use in the East, and communication was sent as far west as Missouri by wire. From there, it would have to be delivered by horse. At the other end of the line, mail could be efficiently transported from Sacramento west to San Francisco by boat through the San Joaquin Delta.

The route would cover 1,966 miles. Hundreds of men were hired to construct the stations along the route. Home stations, where riders were to be posted, were built seventy-five miles apart. Between them, spaced about every fifteen miles, would be smaller stations that housed fresh mounts.

Eighty riders were hired all along the route, many in Carson City, Nevada. These young men had to be fearless and bold and hardened by years of life in the West. They would be paid between $50 and $125 per month, which was a handsome salary at the time.

Alexander Majors was a religious man who grew up in the East. He was astounded when he first heard the vulgarity of some of the men in the Wild West. He made each rider take the following pledge:

> While I am in the employ of A. Majors, I agree not to use profane language, not to get drunk, not to gamble,

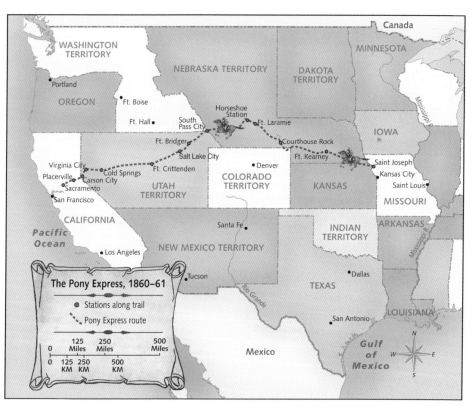

The Pony Express route covered 1,966 miles through flat plains, desert, and rugged mountains. This map shows the route from St. Joseph, Missouri, to Sacramento, California.

not to treat animals cruelly, and not to do anything else that is incompatible with the conduct of a gentleman. And I agree, if I violate any of the above conditions, to accept my discharge without any pay for my services.[2]

Getting Started

The owners named their enterprise the Pony Express because the name sounded good. In reality, ponies were seldom used. Rather, the riders rode full-grown horses ranging from durable California mustangs and cayuses to thoroughbreds from Iowa. They were the best horses money could buy. The owners paid an average of $200 per animal—quite a high price.

The operation was put together in two months without a lot of fanfare. When the *Leavenworth Daily Times* in Kansas learned of the momentous plan, it carried a banner headline that read:

> GREAT EXPRESS ADVENTURE FROM LEAVENWORTH TO SACRAMENTO IN TEN DAYS. CLEAR THE TRACK AND LET THE PONY COME THROUGH.[3]

The trio of Russell, Waddell, and Majors guessed that it would take between ten and twelve days for the mail to run the whole route end to end. This was great news to citizens everywhere. The Great American Desert, as the expanse of the West was sometimes called, would seem less vast. Communication between East and West would greatly improve.

Some doubted the plan would work. They figured there were just too many obstacles. Water would be hard to come by for long stretches. Horses could never make it through the fierce blizzards of the Rocky Mountains or Sierra Nevada. Riders also faced the constant threat of attack by American Indian warriors.

The Pony Express operation was put together in about two months. Although there was little fanfare, some newspapers covered its beginning. This is a poster advertising for the Pony Express.

chapter 3

The Adventure Begins

Finally it was April 3, 1860, the inaugural day of this new mail delivery system. All the questions about the new Pony Express were about to be answered. An immense crowd gathered in the streets of St. Joseph, Missouri, on the momentous day. A big brass band played triumphantly. Flags and banners hung from buildings. Speeches were made by the mayor and by Alexander Majors. A holiday spirit was in the air.[1]

The Westbound Route Opens

The shrill whistle of the *Missouri* rang out as the train pulled into the depot carrying the mail from the East. The pouches were rushed to the post office, where the express mail was sorted and placed in a mochila. The sturdy leather pouch held eighty-five pieces of mail, including a message of congratulations from President James Buchanan. The mochila was hurried out to the Pony Express rider, who threw it over his saddle and climbed aboard.

Historians disagree about the identity of the first rider from St. Joseph. At least seven young men are listed in various books and newspaper accounts as the honored figure, with the most popular two being Billy Richardson and Johnny Fry. Most historians who have researched the matter believe that it was Johnny.[2]

Whoever the mystery rider was, he climbed onto a bright bay mare and trotted her out to the starting point at the Pike's Peak Livery Stables. Spectators plucked hairs from her tail to make souvenir rings and watch chains. The rider demanded that they stop as it was his job to prevent cruelty to the animals. Suddenly, a cannon on the hill above boomed! With that, rider and horse were off to the thunderous cheers of the citizens of St. Joseph.

The bay mare galloped a short distance to the Missouri River wharf where a ferry boat was waiting. Across the river was Elwood, in Kansas Territory. The horse trotted on deck, a whistle tooted, and the ferry carried the horse, rider, and mochila to the other side. The crowd lining the river in St. Joseph roared its

The identity of the first Pony Express rider to leave St. Joseph, Missouri, is unknown, but it is believed to be either Johnny Fry or Billy Richardson. This is a painting of the rider leaving St. Joseph on April 3, 1860.

approval once again. No sooner had the boat reached the other side and the gangplank been lowered than the horse and rider were off in a cloud of dust.

The Eastbound Route Begins

Meanwhile, at the other end of the route in Sacramento, a smaller celebration took place. On a steamer, the eastbound mail had been sent up the Sacramento River from San Francisco, arriving in Sacramento on time. It was a rainy night, but the occasion still was celebrated.

Bells clanged and guns were fired; flags were unfurled and people tossed flowers in the air.

The first rider, William "Sam" Hamilton, tossed the mochila—holding seventy-five pieces of mail—over his saddle. He climbed on his snow-white bronco and away he sped.

William changed horses once as he rode the first twenty miles in fifty-nine minutes. He switched mounts again at Folsom Station and again twice more until he reached Sportsman's Hall, in Placerville, where Warren Upson relieved him. William was proud to have been the first eastbound rider. However, he was glad to step inside the home station of Placerville, for it had rained the entire way.

The next leg of the journey was treacherous, as Warren found out. The terrain went uphill as the route started up the Sierra Nevada Mountains. The air got colder, and the rain turned to snow. Before long, Warren was tramping through heavy white powder. At times, he had to dismount and lead his horse. Brave and determined, he reached the top of the Sierra at Friday's Station, where he passed the precious mochila to Pony Bob Haslam, who carried it down the mountain and into the vast sands of Nevada.

Falling Behind Schedule

Meanwhile, the westbound mail was behind schedule. The mochila had been transferred three times until it was in the hands of Henry Wallace, who arrived at Fort Kearney, in what is now Nebraska. From there, Joseph Barney Wintle carried it to Cottonwood Springs. From rider to rider it went, through muddy trails, across swollen streams, until it reached the base of the Rocky Mountains. Then the mochila was carried up through South Pass, and on to Fort Bridger. It was somewhere along this point that the eastbound and westbound mails passed. "Hoooooo!" the riders yelled. They raised their hats as they whizzed by one another, not even stopping to exchange trail conditions.

At 6:25 P.M. on April 9, the westbound rider arrived in Salt Lake City. Richard Egan took the mochila and rushed it seventy-five miles to Rush Valley. William Dennis advanced it to Egan Canyon. William Fisher took it to Ruby Valley.

The eastbound mochila was sped past Fort Laramie, Scott's Bluff, and Courthouse Rock. The rains had been heavy for days, and when the rider reached the bank of the Platte River, he found it swollen.

The rider plunged in to make the crossing anyway. Not more than three strides out, the horse was swept off its feet and was carried downstream into treacherous quicksand. The rider ripped the mochila from his saddle and swam ashore. Without a second to lose, he borrowed a horse from a bystander and dashed on. The horse in the quicksand was rescued. The mail was passed along to four more riders until it reached the hands of Johnny Fry, who was waiting to carry it on to St. Joseph.

Four hours later, Johnny urged his steed onto the ferryboat that would escort him across the Missouri

A celebration in Sacramento to honor the arrival of the first Pony Express rider from St. Joseph on April 13, 1860.

River to St. Joseph. At 5:00 P.M. on April 13, Johnny guided his horse through cheering crowds and dismounted outside the mail office. The mochila had arrived on schedule.

A Joyous Celebration

That night, the town staged a wild celebration. Uniformed militiamen paraded up and down the streets, cheerfully shooting their muskets into the air. Bonfires roared, fireworks exploded, and the cannon that had signaled the start of the Pony Express ten days earlier was fired again and again.[3]

In Sacramento, a celebration of equal magnitude took place. Billy Hamilton had taken the westbound mochila the final seventy-five miles to the state capital, where it arrived at 5:25 P.M. Billy was escorted down Fort Sutter Road to J Street by nearly a hundred horsemen. He dismounted in front of the Express office and raised the mailbag above his head as the crowd roared. Handkerchiefs and hats were waved, and a cannon boomed forty times.[4]

The Pony Express riders had proved that they could do it—they could deliver the mail. Now the question was, could they keep it up?

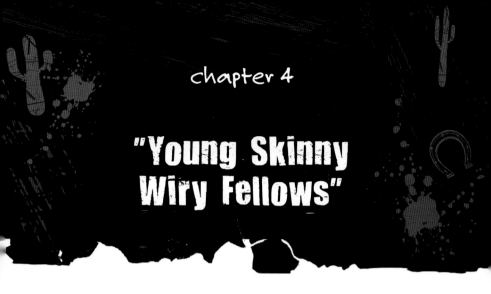

chapter 4

"Young Skinny Wiry Fellows"

The riders of the Pony Express had to have special qualities. The advertisement in the San Francisco newspapers in March 1860, spelled it out this way: "YOUNG SKINNY WIRY FELLOWS not over eighteen. Must be expert riders willing to risk death daily. Orphans preferred. Wages $25 per week. Apply, Central Overland Express, Alta Bldg., Montgomery St."[1]

Hundreds of young men across the country applied. Eighty were carefully chosen. The Pony Express would employ only the best riders in the West to deliver the mail.

The Job of Each Rider

The riders were posted at stations along a route that stretched across the West—from St. Joseph, Missouri, to Sacramento, California. It was each rider's job to travel at breakneck speed from one station to the next, about seventy-five miles, where he would pass the mochila to the next rider.

The route traversed rugged mountains and crossed blistering deserts. The riders had to fight through paralyzing heat, rainstorms, blizzards, outlaw attacks, and, of course, the hostile American Indians whose homes were being invaded. They risked life and limb to uphold the code of the Pony Express: "The U.S. Mail must and will go through."[2]

Despite the success of the first rides, and all the fuss that was made over them, many people still doubted the reliability of the Pony Express. One newspaper even claimed that the operation was "simply inviting slaughter upon all the foolhardy young men who had been engaged as riders."[3]

William F. Cody

But the Pony Express riders were brave, smart, and resourceful. They generally were teenagers, weighed no more than 150 pounds, and had several years of experience in riding. Well, most of them, anyway. One boy walked into Horseshoe Station in Nebraska Territory one day, wearing a dirty shirt and jeans, worn-out boots, and a shabby cowboy hat. "I want a job, riding mail," he announced.

Joe Slade, the rugged station agent behind the desk, laughed and said, "Come back, say, in five years."

"I want that job now," the boy demanded.

"Shucks! You ain't a day over fourteen," Joe said.

"You're a liar," the boy snapped, and he whipped out his revolver. "You take that back!"

The man paused a moment to look the boy over. He liked what he saw. "You ride?" the man asked.

"Anything you can cinch a saddle on."

"You're hired."[4]

With that, William F. "Buffalo Bill" Cody became one of the youngest riders in the Pony Express. He was just fourteen. Age didn't matter, though, as Buffalo Bill proved to be a great rider.

Riding into the Three Crossings Station one day after a run of some 116 miles from Red Buttes, Buffalo Bill found that his relief rider had been killed in a barroom brawl. Bill pleaded to take the precious mochila seventy-six miles west to the next home station, Rocky Ridge.

"It was a very bad and dangerous country, but the emergency was so great," Bill later said.[5] He arrived at

A portrait of Buffalo Bill Cody taken at age nineteen. Bill joined the Pony Express as a rider at age fourteen.

Rocky Ridge just as the eastbound mochila was brought in. Exhausted, but eager to prove his value, Bill saddled a fresh horse and sped off eastward. He retraced his steps clear back to Red Buttes. He covered a distance of 384 miles—a Pony Express record!

The Riders

Riders came from all walks of life. Alexander Toponce came to the United States with his parents from France when he was seven. He worked as a freight and stagecoach driver in Missouri before joining the Pony Express at twenty-one. Elijah Nichols Wilson lived among the Shoshone for two years before becoming a Pony Express rider. Elijah H. Maxfield was a lumber-jack who cut and hauled timber in the Utah Territory. William Page traveled from England with his parents to the Utah Territory where he repaired guns for Brigham Young.

There was no official outfit for riders. A rider often wore a buckskin shirt, ordinary pants tucked into high boots, and a slouch hat or cap. The mailbags were light leather pouches that were usually kept locked.

The Station House

Riders were required to stay within a hundred yards of the station at all times. One rider said, "We had to be ready to start back at a half-minute's notice, let it be day or night, rain or shine."[6] It was the station keeper's duty to have a horse saddled and ready to go half an hour before a rider's expected arrival.

Riders spent most of their time between runs sleeping. Each station had a bed reserved especially for them. Sometimes they could sleep just a few hours before they had to ride again. When there was a delay

Station houses were a welcome sign of relief for Pony Express riders. The station house meant rest and food. This Pony Express rider is preparing to leave a station house.

of a day or more between runs, riders would help the station keeper tend the horses, or just relax by reading or playing cards.

Animal Cruelty

The riders' first priority was to get the mail through on time. Sometimes, this led to cruel treatment of the horses. To encourage riders to make good time, a Pony Express agent once told them, "Boys, if you kill a horse by riding fast we will buy a better one."[7]

Richard Egan was speeding along one day on a beautiful horse when the animal missed its footing and fell, breaking its neck. Richard ripped the mochila from his saddle and ran the last five miles of his route. He received a hero's welcome when he finally reached his destination.

Record Time

The best record made by the Pony Express was when a telegram containing President Abraham Lincoln's inaugural speech was delivered in March of 1861. The nation was on the verge of civil war, and citizens across the West were eager for inspiring words from the great president. Express riders sensed the urgency, and pushed their horses on faster than ever before. The telegram was carried from St. Joseph to Sacramento in just seven days and seventeen hours. It was another heroic accomplishment by the riders of the Pony Express.

chapter 5

Overcoming the Wilderness

R iders had to overcome many hazards along the route. The terrain was especially rugged through the Rocky Mountains in Wyoming Territory and in the Sierra Nevada Mountains of California between Placerville and Friday's Station. Trail conditions worsened in bad weather.

Blizzard

William Fisher was so exhausted in a blizzard one night that he dismounted and stretched out in the snow to sleep. He would have frozen to death if a rabbit hadn't come along and jumped on his legs, waking him up.

George Little was caught once in storm so severe that he had to leave his horse, which could no longer trudge through the heavy snow. George cut open the

When Pony Express riders had to cross the mountains, weather conditions could be treacherous. Blizzards could cause snow to cover the trails, making travel almost impossible.

mailbag with his pocketknife and stuffed all the letters under his shirt. He then forged a trail through deep snow over a mountain to reach a relay station the next morning. From there, he rode a horse bareback into Salt Lake City. The townspeople were so elated to see the mail stashed under George's shirt that they carried him around the street on their shoulders.

Richard Egan set out from Salt Lake City one night in a blizzard; he was bound for Fort Crittenden, some forty miles to the west. The snow was knee-deep to the horse, and Richard could not see the trail. He rode according to the wind.

"It was striking on my right cheek so I kept it there, but unfortunately for me, the wind changed and led me off my course," he said. "Instead of going westward I went southward and rode all night on a high trot, and arrived at the place I had left at sundown the evening before."[1] Richard finally reached Fort Crittenden, but not before traveling more than 150 miles and nearly freezing to death.

The American Indians

American Indians posed a major threat to the Pony Express operation. With the rush to find gold and the arrival of thousands of white settlers, the American Indians were losing their land. In an effort to protect their territory from invasion, warriors sometimes attacked the riders or the station houses.

After one month of on-time delivery, rider Tom Flynn approached Williams Station from the west in full gallop. He planned to switch horses and go on. But as Tom neared the station, he noticed that his fresh mount, normally saddled and ready to go, was not outside. The station keepers were nowhere to be seen.

As white settlers moved west and claimed control over American Indian territory, many American Indians, such as the Paiute, fought to defend their land. This photo of Paiute men, women, and children shows them wearing traditional dress.

Tom brought his horse to a stop in front of the station and gasped with horror. The station keepers were stretched out on the ground, their bodies riddled with arrows. Tom trembled with fear as he mounted his horse and urged it on. He reached Virginia City and reported the news. There were several more attacks that day. Home stations strung across what is now Nevada and western Utah were wide open to attack. The Pony Express was immediately halted.

Mail piled up for three weeks in San Francisco and Salt Lake City until enough soldiers were in place to fully protect the station keepers and riders. Only then did the operation resume. The Paiute kept up the attack. Relay stations were torched, and horses were stolen. The U.S. Army provided better protection, but it wasn't always available.

Albert Armstrong and Henry Woodville Wilson were station keepers at the one-room log cabin in Egan Canyon. One morning after breakfast, Albert heard moaning noises outside the cabin. He peeked through the window at a sight that sent a chill through his spine. "My God, Wood," he shrieked, "it's Indians!"[2] Outside was an entire band of war-painted Paiute.

Albert and Henry grabbed their shotguns, dropped to the floor, and opened fire through cracks in the wall. The yelling warriors raced around to the back. The desperate station keepers continued firing until their ammunition had run out, then the Paiute burst through the door. Albert and Henry were backed up to the far wall, knives in hand, prepared to fight to the death. Before the attackers could kill the station keepers, the

Paiute chief was at the doorway, standing with folded arms. "Bread!" he commanded.[3]

At first, Albert and Henry didn't know what to think. After the chief kept pointing at several loaves of bread on a table, the station keepers understood. They eagerly handed the bread to the hungry warriors. The chief gestured to the sacks of flour on the floor. Again, the station keepers understood. They mixed dough and baked more bread for the Paiute. This continued all day. What would the warriors do to them when there was no more bread? Finally, the last sack of flour was empty.

The station keepers were dragged outside. A wagon tongue was detached and driven into the ground. Sagebrush was gathered. Albert and Henry knew their fate now. They would be burned at the stake. The warriors gathered around in a circle.

Just then, a rumble of hoofbeats could be heard. It grew louder and louder until it became a thunderous stampede. Express rider William Dennis had come by the station house earlier and had seen the commotion inside. He notified a nearby contingent of U.S. cavalrymen, who sped to the rescue. Led by Colonel E. J. Steptoe, the cavalrymen sent the Paiute in every direction. Albert and Henry were saved.

Thieves and Bandits

American Indians weren't the only threat to the riders. Bandits lurked along the route and could strike at any time. Sometimes they wanted the horse, sometimes they wanted the mail.

Melvin Baughn once had his horse stolen while he was riding. He followed the thief on foot for some distance, attacked him at the right moment, and reclaimed his horse to complete the ride.

Buffalo Bill Cody learned one night that a large sum of money was in the mochila he was to carry. He stuffed wads of paper in another mochila and draped it over his saddle in normal fashion. He hid the mochila with the money under a saddle blanket. On the route, Buffalo Bill was held up by two men. "You'll hang for this," Bill said.

"We'll take our chances on that," one of the bandits said. "Hand over the mailbag."[4]

Buffalo Bill tossed the paper-stuffed mochila at the highwaymen, and at the same time he drew his revolver and shot one of them in the arm. He spurred on his horse as the other outlaw sent a bullet whizzing past his ear. Bill arrived safely at the next station with the real mochila and the money. It was this sort of resourcefulness that made the Pony Express a success.

chapter 6

Farewell and Forever

On the fateful day of April 12, 1861, cannonballs rocked the walls of Fort Sumter, South Carolina. The Civil War had begun. Pony Express riders dashed back and forth across the West with news of the war between the North and South. The government in Washington, D.C., insisted that the Express operation be kept in top form. The national government wanted to maintain solid communication with California to keep the valuable state loyal to the cause of the North.

Everyone associated with the Pony Express knew that it would not last forever. The United States was still less than a century old, and progress moved as swiftly as the Express horses. Wagon trains had replaced steamships. The Pony Express had replaced the wagon train. Surely, another operation was bound to replace the Pony Express. That operation would turn out to be a long wire—the telegraph.

The Pony Express was a creative success—but a financial failure. The founding trio of Russell, Majors, and Waddell invested $700,000 in the operation and earned only $500,000. In early 1861, the three men went bankrupt and were forced to sell the company.

The government supported the Pony Express for a time. Then the stagecoach became a more affordable means of mail delivery. The Express was faster, but more people preferred to use the stagecoach—that is, until the emergence of the telegraph.

A telegraph could flash messages from end to end in seconds. A network of electrical lines weaved through the eastern states, stretching as far west as St. Joseph. The government decided that it was time to expand those communication lines.

Poles were raised and wires were strung simultaneously from San Francisco eastward and St. Joseph westward. The end was near for the Pony Express. The Express continued its run—just at a shorter distance now—from Carson City to Fort Laramie. Through the summer of 1861, the riders hurtled past workers erecting poles in the desert.

A Pony Express rider gallops past men constructing a telegraph line. The telegraph signaled the end for the Pony Express.

The two strings of wires inched closer together, where they would be joined in Salt Lake City. On September 11, the first poles began to appear on Main Street. On October 17, the wires were connected. On October 18, the first message by wire was sent from Salt Lake City by Brigham Young to the president of the Western Union Telegraph Company offering hearty congratulations. On October 24, the Pony Express was discontinued.

No congratulations were sent to the Pony Express. For the next three years, the Civil War demanded the attention of all Americans. The operation, after all it had accomplished, quietly closed down. Some relay stations were torn down; others crumbled into decay. Horses were sold, and riders found new jobs. The memory of the Express faded.

The news account in the *Sacramento Bee* on October 26, 1861, opened its report this way: "Our little friend, the Pony, is to run no more. Farewell and forever, thou staunch, wilderness-overcoming, swift-footed messenger."[1]

The Pony Express lasted eighteen months. In that time, the gallant riders covered a distance of 616,000 miles. Through blizzards and mud, rivers and floods—and worse—they rode. The mochila was lost only once. The stories of the brave riders of the Pony Express will never be lost.

NOTICE.

BY ORDERS FROM THE EAST,

THE PONY EXPRESS

WILL be DISCONTINUED.

The Last Pony coming this way left Atchison, Kansas, yesterday.

oc25-1t   WELLS, FARGO & CO., Agents.

On October 24, 1861, the Pony Express was shut down. Newspapers spread the word around the country. Although the Pony Express lasted less than two years, its legacy would live on in American history.

Chapter Notes

Chapter 1. The Mail Must and Will Go Through

1. Tom West, *Heroes on Horseback* (New York: Four Winds Press, 1969), p. 15.
2. Ibid., p. 16.
3. Kate B. Carter, *Riders of the Pony Express* (Salt Lake City: Pony Express Memorial Commision of Utah, 1952), p. 22.
4. West, p. 18.
5. Ibid.
6. Ibid., p. 19.

Chapter 2. A Great Express Adventure

1. Raymond W. Settle, *Saddles and Spurs* (Harrisburg, Pa.: The Stackpole Company, 1955), p. 32.
2. Roy S. Bloss, *Pony Express—The Great Gamble* (Berkeley, Calif.: Howell-North Press, 1959), p. 95.
3. Settle, p. 35.

Chapter 3. The Adventure Begins

1. Arthur Chapman, *Pony Express* (New York: A. L. Burt Company, 1932), pp. 91–109.
2. William H. Floyd, *Phantom Riders of the Pony Express* (Philadelphia: Dorrance & Company, 1958), pp. 53–64.
3. Raymond W. Settle, *Saddles and Spurs* (Harrisburg, Pa.: The Stackpole Company, 1955), pp. 44–51.
4. Ibid.

Chapter 4. "Young Skinny Wiry Fellows"

1. Gene Morgan, *Westward the Course of Empire* (Chicago: The Lakeside Press, 1945), p. 5.
2. Ibid., p. 16.
3. Waddell F. Smith, *The Story of the Pony Express* (San Rafael, Calif.: Pony Express History and Art Gallery, 1960), p. 14.
4. Tom West, *Heroes on Horseback* (New York: Four Winds Press, 1969), p. 33.
5. Roy S. Bloss, *Pony Express—The Great Gamble* (Berkeley, Calif.: Howell-North Press, 1959), p. 101.
6. Kate B. Carter, *Riders of the Pony Express* (Salt Lake City: Pony Express Memorial Commision of Utah, 1952), p. 31.
7. Ibid., p. 19.

Chapter 5. Overcoming the Wilderness

1. Kate B. Carter, *Riders of the Pony Express* (Salt Lake City: Pony Express Memorial Commision of Utah, 1952), p. 19.
2. Roy S. Bloss, *Pony Express—The Great Gamble* (Berkeley, Calif.: Howell-North Press, 1959), p. 97.
3. Tom West, *Heroes on Horseback* (New York: Four Winds Press, 1969), p. 66.
4. Gene Morgan, *Westward the Course of Empire* (Chicago: The Lakeside Press, 1945), p. 49.

Chapter 6. Farewell and Forever

1. Waddell F. Smith, *The Story of the Pony Express* (San Rafael, Calif.: Pony Express History and Art Gallery, 1960), p. 90.

Glossary

alkali wastes—A dried-out desert lake, containing large amounts of salt.

bankrupt—A person or company judged by a court to be insolvent, or unable to pay outstanding debts.

cayuse—An American Indian pony.

Civil War—The war fought between the northern (Union) states and the southern (Confederate) states from 1861 to 1865.

delta—Land built from silt at the mouth of a river.

enterprise—A business venture.

highwayman—A thief who preys on travelers.

immigrants—People who enter a country or territory from another country or territory.

inaugural address—The speech given by elected officials after they have taken the oath of office.

isthmus—A narrow strip of land between two large bodies of water. The Isthmus of Panama separates the Atlantic and Pacific oceans.

mochila—The mailbag used by the Pony Express. It was slung over the back of the horse like a saddle. On each side of the mochila, there were two pockets.

mustang—A small, hardy wild horse of the North American plains, descended from Arabian horses brought to America by Spanish explorers.

slouch hat—A soft felt hat with a flexible brim.

stampede—A sudden uncontrolled rush of cattle or other herd animals.

telegraph—A system of communication where clicks are transmitted hundreds of miles over wires. In 1862, the first transcontinental wire was completed.

Further Reading

Books

Gunderson, Jessica. *Young Riders of the Pony Express.* Mankato, Minn.: Capstone Press, 2006.

McNeese, Tim. *The Pony Express: Bringing Mail to the American West.* New York: Chelsea House Publishers, 2009.

Rau, Margaret. *The Mail Must Go Through: The Story of the Pony Express.* Greensboro, N.C.: Morgan Reynolds Publishing, 2005.

Spradlin, Michael P. *Off Like the Wind!: The First Ride of the Pony Express.* New York: Walker, 2010.

Thompson, Gare. *Riding With the Mail: The Story of the Pony Express.* Washington, D.C.: National Geographic, 2007.

Internet Addresses

The Gold Rush Chronicles: The Pony Express
<http://comspark.com/chronicles/ponyexpress.htm>

Pony Express Museum
<http://www.ponyexpress.org/>

U.S. National Park Service: Pony Express National Historic Trail
<http://www.nps.gov/poex/index.htm>

Index

A

American Indians,
5–11, 26, 34–37
animal cruelty, 14–15,
30–31
Armstrong, Albert,
36–37

B

bandits, thieves, 38
blizzards, 16, 26,
32–34
Buchanan, James, 19
Butterfield, John, 13
Butterfield Overland
Mail Company, 13

C

Civil War, 39–42
Cody, William F.
"Buffalo Bill,"
26–28, 38

D

Dennis, William, 22,
37

E

Egan, Richard, 22,
30–31, 33–34

F

Fisher, William, 22, 32
Flynn, Tom, 34–35
Fry, Johnny, 19, 23–24

H

Hamilton, William
"Sam," 21, 24

Haslam, Bob "Pony
Bob," 5–11, 21
horses, 9, 14–16,
30–31, 38

K

King, Tom, 6–7, 11

L

Lincoln, Abraham, 31
Little, George, 32–33

M

Majors, Alexander,
13–16, 18, 40
Maxfield, Elijah H., 29
mochilas, 18–19

P

Page, William, 29
Pony Express
celebration of, 18,
20, 24
eastbound route,
20–24
funding of, 13, 40
generally, 12–17,
39–42
profitability, 40
records, 28, 31
schedule, keeping,
22–24
westbound route,
18–20, 22

R

railroads, 12
Richardson, Billy, 19
riders
dangers to, 5–11,

16, 21–23, 26,
32–38
dedication of, 5–11
job of, 5–11, 25–26
pledge, 14–15
qualities of, 25,
28–29
salaries, 14
Russell, William H.,
13–16, 40

S

stagecoaches, 13, 28,
40
station houses, 14,
29–30
steamships, 12, 39

T

telegraph, 14, 40–41
Toponce, Alexander,
28–29

W

Waddell, William B.,
13–16, 40
Wallace, Henry, 22
Wilson, Elijah Nichols,
29
Wilson, Henry
Woodville, 36–37
Wintle, Joseph Barney,
22